W9-AKD-286

Unsolved!

MYSTERIOUS PREDICTIONS

Kathryn Walker

based on original text by Brian Innes

Crabtree Publishing Company

www.crabtreebooks.com

Crabtree Publishing Company

www.crabtreebooks.com

Author: Kathryn Walker
    based on original text by Brian Innes
Project editor: Kathryn Walker
Picture researcher: Rachel Tisdale
Managing editor: Miranda Smith
Art director: Jeni Child
Designer: Rob Norridge
Design manager: David Poole
Editorial director: Lindsey Lowe
Children's publisher: Anne O'Daly
Editor: Molly Aloian
Proofreader: Crystal Sikkens
Crabtree editorial director: Kathy Middleton
Production coordinator: Katherine Berti
Prepress technician: Katherine Berti

Cover: Some people believe crystal balls
can be used to predict the future.

Photographs:
Corbis: Christie's Images: p. 13
Fortean Picture Library: p. 26–27
Getty Images: Hulton Archive: p. 25;
    Popperfoto: p. 10–11; Three Lions:
    p. 17; Time Life Pictures: p. 24
Istockphoto: Christophe Testi: p. 7
Mary Evans Picture Library: p. 9, 19
Science Photo Library: Oscar Burriel:
    front cover
Shutterstock: Michael D. Brown: p. 30;
    Albert de Bruijn: p. 8; Gertjan Hooijer:
    p. 4–5, 6–7; Maisei Raman: p. 22;
    Schmid Christophe: p. 23; Jurgen
    Ziewe: p. 20–21, 28–29
Topham: p. 12, 15, 18
Wikipedia Commons: p. 16

Every effort has been made to trace
the owners of copyrighted material.

Library and Archives Canada Cataloguing in Publication

Walker, Kathryn, 1957-
    Mysterious predictions / Kathryn Walker ; based on
original text by Brian Innes.

(Unsolved!)
Includes index.
ISBN 978-0-7787-4151-0 (bound).--ISBN 978-0-7787-4164-0 (pbk.)

    1. Prophecies (Occultism)--Juvenile literature. I. Innes, Brian
II. Title. III. Series: Unsolved! (St. Catharines, Ont.)

BF1791.W34 2009   j133.3   C2009-901927-2

Library of Congress Cataloging-in-Publication Data

Walker, Kathryn.
    Mysterious predictions / Kathryn Walker ; based on original text by
Brian Innes.
      p. cm. -- (Unsolved!)
    Includes index.
    ISBN 978-0-7787-4164-0 (pbk. : alk. paper) -- ISBN 978-0-7787-4151-0
(reinforced library binding : alk. paper)
    1. Prophecies (Occultism)--Juvenile literature. pre I. Innes, Brian. II. Title.
III. Series.

    BF1791.W36 2010
    133.3--dc22

                                      2009013081

Crabtree Publishing Company

www.crabtreebooks.com   1-800-387-7650

Published in Canada
Crabtree Publishing
616 Welland Ave.
St. Catharines, ON
L2M 5V6

Published in the United States
Crabtree Publishing
PMB16A
350 Fifth Ave., Suite 3308
New York, NY 10118

Published by **CRABTREE PUBLISHING COMPANY** in 2010

Contents

When Dreams Come True

...Some dreams seem to show the future.

On March 8, 1946, John Godley in Oxford, England had a strange dream. He dreamed he was reading the next day's evening newspaper. In it, he saw the results of the day's horse racing.

When he woke, Godley could remember the names of two winning horses—Bindal and Juladin. He checked and found that those horses were indeed running that day. He and his friends **bet** money on them winning. The dream came true.

Godley had several more dreams of winning horses. But after about three years, the dreams stopped. In 1958, he dreamed that "What Man?" won the world-famous Grand National race. It turned out that a horse named "Mr. What" was running in it. Godley bet on the horse and won a large sum of money.

John Godley, a student in Oxford, found he could dream the names of winning racehorses.

>> **bet**—To gamble or risk money on the result of an event or race

"When he woke, Godley could remember the names of two winning horses..."

How Strange...

There were times when Godley got the horses' names slightly wrong. He once dreamed of a winner named "Tubermore" when its name was really "Tuberose."

To prove his story, Godley wrote down a dream about two horses. He put the sheet of paper in an envelope. It was **timestamped** and sealed by the post office. Both the horses won.

A recurring dream

David Booth was an office worker in Cincinnati, Ohio. In May 1979, he had the same dreadful dream ten nights in a row. In it, Booth saw a three-engine American Airlines jet taking off at an airport. Then he saw it flip over and explode. Booth said it was "like watching television."

Horrified, Booth called American Airlines on May 22. The airline took his dream seriously, but there was nothing they could do—they needed more information to prevent such an accident from occurring.

On May 25, an American Airlines DC-10 took off from O'Hare Airport, Chicago. The plane lifted off the ground, then turned over and exploded, killing 273 people.

How Strange...

 In the early 1900s, engineer John William Dunne studied dreams and time. He suggested that people were able to **experience** the past, present, and future in dreams.

In his dreams, David Booth saw a plane, similar to this, crash just after takeoff.

>> **experience**—To live through or take part in something

This picture shows the twin towers of the World Trade Center before the terrorist attack of 2001.

Nightmare

Englishwoman Valerie Clarke claimed she was a psychic. A psychic is someone who has unexplained powers of the mind. In June 2001, Valerie appeared on British television in a chat show called "Kilroy."

Valerie told the host she had dreamed about a bombing at the World Trade Center in New York. In her dream, she saw the building blow up. She said, "At the same time, this plane went down behind it [the World Trade Center]. I was not sure if the plane had gone into the building."

Three months later, **terrorists** flew two Boeing 767 jets into the twin towers of the World Trade Center, killing 2,749 people.

>> **terrorist**—Someone who uses violence as a political weapon

Dream at the White House

One April night in 1865, President Abraham Lincoln had a vivid dream. He told his wife and friends, "Although it was only a dream, I have been strangely annoyed by it ever since."

Lincoln dreamed he was woken by sobbing. He got out of bed to investigate. In the East Room of the White House, he saw soldiers guarding a body. A crowd of people were weeping. Lincoln asked a soldier "Who is dead in the White House?" "The president," answered the soldier, "He was killed by an **assassin**." A loud cry of grief from the crowd woke Lincoln from his dream.

A few days later, on April 14, Lincoln visited Ford's Theater in Washington, D.C. There he was shot by actor John Wilkes Booth. He died the following day.

"'Although it was only a dream, I have been strangely annoyed by it ever since.'"

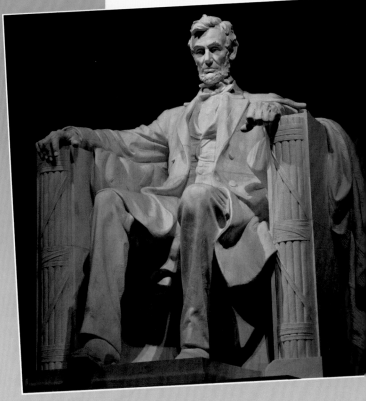

This statue of Abraham Lincoln forms part of the Lincoln Memorial in Washington, D.C.

>> **assassin**—Someone who carries out a murder for political reasons

The peddler's dream

A much happier dream is remembered by the townspeople of Swaffham in Norfolk, England. In the 1400s, a **peddler** named John Chapman dreamed he should go to London Bridge where he would hear good news. Chapman walked 100 miles (160 kilometers) to London. He waited on the bridge for three days, but nothing happened.

As Chapman turned to go home, a shopkeeper asked him what he had been waiting for. When Chapman told the shopkeeper about his dream, he laughed. The shopkeeper said that if he believed in dreams he would be in a place called Swaffham. He had dreamed that gold was hidden there. It was buried under a tree in a peddler's garden.

Chapman went home and found two pots of gold buried under his tree. He used some of the gold to help build a new church in Swaffham.

John Chapman is pictured here on the left, talking to a man on London Bridge.

Sense of Doom

...People sometimes sense that bad things are about to happen.

Eryl Mai Jones lived in the coal-mining town of Aberfan in Wales. One day in October 1966, the ten-year-old told her mother: "I'm not afraid to die." Her mother said she was too young to talk of dying. "But I shall be with my friends," Eryl replied. On October 20, Eryl had a dream. She told her mother, "I went to school, and there was no school there. Something black had come down all over it."

On October 21, Eryl went off to elementary school in Aberfan. At 9:15 A.M. a 500,000-ton (450,000-tonne) heap of coal-mining **waste** slid down from a hill above the school. The wet, black waste poured into the classrooms. It killed 144 people, most of them schoolchildren.

Eryl's body was dug out of the waste. She was laid to rest alongside the bodies of her friends.

How Strange...

It was reported that some of the other children who died in the disaster had dreams similar to Eryl's.

Other people in Aberfan had growing feelings of **anxiety** in the weeks before the disaster.

>> **waste**—Material that is unusable or unwanted

The scene at Aberfan on October 21, 1966. Coal waste from a mountain crashed down on the town, destroying the elementary school (the building at the center of the photo).

More premonitions

There were a lot of people who claimed they had premonitions of the Aberfan disaster. A premonition is when someone has a dream, vision, or feeling warning them of something that will happen. Dr. J.C. Barker investigated these claims. He found that in 24 cases, the dreams had been told to other people before the disaster happened.

Mrs. Grace Engleton was one of these cases. She lived more than 300 miles (480 km) from Aberfan and had never been to Wales. On October 14, she clearly dreamed of a coal-mining village. She saw coal and water hurtle down a mountain and bury a schoolhouse. A neighbor said Mrs. Engleton had told her about the dream four days before the **tragedy**.

"'...[Mrs Engleton] saw coal and water hurtle down a mountain and bury a schoolhouse."

One survivor of the Aberfan disaster is carried to safety.

>> **tragedy**—A shocking and very sad event

The Titanic

Reports of many strange premonitions surround the sinking of the ship *Titanic*. On the night of April 14, 1912, the British **liner** sank after striking an iceberg in the Atlantic Ocean. About 1,500 lives were lost.

Blanche Marshall lived near the launch site of the *Titanic*. As she and her family watched it leave, she cried out "That ship is going to sink...Do something!...You fools, I can see hundreds of people struggling in the icy waters."

In 1898, a novel by Morgan Robertson had been published. It told the story of a great ocean liner named *Titan*. During an April voyage, *Titan* struck an iceberg and sank, causing many deaths. Details of the liner, its speed, and the number of people on board were eerily close to those of the *Titanic*.

At the time of its voyage, the Titanic *(shown here) was the largest and most luxurious ship afloat. People thought it was unsinkable.*

Prophecies

...Throughout history, people have made prophecies.

A prophecy is a **prediction** of future events in the form of a message. In ancient times, prophecies were believed to be messages from a god or gods.

One of the most famous writers of prophecies was Michel de Nostredame, better known as Nostradamus. He was born in southern France in 1503. Between 1555 and 1558, Nostradamus published his book titled *The Prophecies*. The book is a collection of prophecies written as four-line **verses**. He deliberately wrote his prophecies in a way that is hard to understand. Nostradamus did not wish to upset people who could do him harm.

Some of Nostradamus' predictions seemed to come true during his lifetime. Ever since, people have searched his verses for meanings. Many believe they have found prophecies of events, such as the two world wars, the death of Diana, Princess of Wales, and the recent war in Iraq.

How Strange.

The queen of France believed Nostradamus had predicted the death of her husband, King Henri II, who died in 1559.

On the night of July 1, 1566, Nostradamus told his assistant "You will not find me alive by sunrise." He died that night.

>> **prediction**—A warning or statement of what will happen in the future

This picture shows Nostradamus writing his predictions. In the background are some of the famous people who these predictions may have concerned.

A life foretold

One of Nostradamus' predictions is believed to be about Queen Elizabeth I of England. It reads:

*She chased out will return
to the kingdom,
Her enemies found to be
conspirators [plotters]:
More than ever her time
will **triumph**,
Three and seventy to death
very sure.*

Elizabeth had many enemies who tried to stop her from becoming queen. But she took the throne in 1558 and her rule was seen as a great success, or "triumph." Elizabeth died at the age of 70 in the year 1603. Some think that the "three" refers to the year in which she died.

Queen Elizabeth I, pictured here, had a long and successful rule. But many people did not want her to become queen.

However, many of Nostradamus' predictions are less clear. Because of this lack of clarity, they can be read to mean different things. Also, some of the predictions did not come true. For example, one verse predicted that a "king of terror" would come from the sky in 1999. This prediction has not come true.

>> **triumph**—Great success or victory

Warning of war

Centuries later, another Frenchman made prophecies that came true. World War I broke out in August 1914. Soon afterward, some German soldiers captured a man in Alsace, France. This prisoner said some strange things. Andreas Rill was one of the soldiers. He wrote a letter to his family about what happened.

According to Rill, the Frenchman told the soldiers: "Throw down your guns! The war will end in 1918 with defeat for the German nation." He went on to predict that a **tyrant** would lead Germany into another war in 1939. But six years later, Germany would again be crushed.

All these things came true. World War I ended in 1918 with Germany defeated. Then in 1939, Adolf Hitler led Germany into World War II. Six years later, Germany was again defeated. No one knows who the mysterious Frenchman was.

"'Throw down your guns! The war will end in 1918 with defeat for the German nation.'"

German troops are here seen marching into Prague, capital of Czechoslovakia, during the build-up to World War II.

A modern-day prophecy

Jeane Dixon was born in Wisconsin, in 1904. She became famous for her prophecies. Jeane said that most of the prophecies came to her in dreams or visions (pictures in the mind).

In May 1956, *Parade* magazine printed an article about Jeane. It reported that she had correctly predicted the results of all presidential elections since 1948. It also said Jeane was predicting that a **Democrat** would win the 1960 election. But she said that while he was president, he would be assassinated or die.

In 1960, Democrat John F. Kennedy became 35th president of the United States. He was assassinated on November 22, 1963.

How Strange...

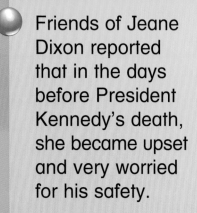

- Friends of Jeane Dixon reported that in the days before President Kennedy's death, she became upset and very worried for his safety.

- In 1942, Jeane warned actress Carole Lombard that it was not safe for her to travel by plane for a few weeks. Days later, the actress died in a plane crash.

Jeane Dixon made some surprising prophecies. She was best known for predicting the death of John F. Kennedy.

>> **Democrat**—A member of the Democratic party of the United States

Another killing

In 1968, Jeane gave a talk at the Ambassador Hotel in Los Angeles. At the time, Robert Kennedy (brother of John F. Kennedy) was running for president. Someone asked Jeane if Robert would ever become president. She replied that he would not "...because of a tragedy right here in this hotel." One week later, Robert Kennedy was shot in the Ambassador Hotel. He died the next day.

Jeane Dixon made thousands of predictions over the years. Many did not come true. For example, she wrongly predicted that World War III would start in 1958 and that Russians would be the first to land on the Moon.

Jeane once said that when her predictions were wrong, it was not because the things she saw happening were wrong. It was because she had **misunderstood** their meaning.

"Jeane Dixon made thousands of predictions over the years."

President John F. Kennedy (right) is pictured here with Robert Kennedy (left). Both brothers were assassinated in the 1960s.

>> **misunderstood**—Understood incorrectly

Written in the Stars

...One popular way of predicting the future is through astrology.

For thousands of years, people have believed that the movement of the planets affects events on Earth and people's lives. Astrology is a way of predicting events through the study of the positions of the planets.

The **influence** that planets have on a person's life is believed to be strongest at the moment of his or her birth. To work out exactly how the planets will influence someone, an astrologer will draw up a special **chart** called a horoscope.

A horoscope shows the position of the Sun, Moon, planets, and stars at the time of birth. An astrologer uses this chart to reveal the person's character and to predict events in his or her life.

>> **influence**—The power to affect someone or something

How Strange...

- In the past, even scientists believed in and practiced astrology.

- Rulers would often take advice from astrologers on important matters.

Astrologers believe they can predict someone's future by studying the positions of the planets, Sun, Moon, and stars.

Constellations

A group of stars is known as a constellation. Early astrologers pictured each constellation as an animal, character, or object. They named it for this picture, for example Pisces (the fish), Libra (the scales), Gemini (the twins), and so on.

Astrologers saw the constellations as forming an imaginary belt called the zodiac. This was divided into 12 sections by 12 constellations. The zodiac seemed like a fixed background against which the planets, Sun, and Moon appeared to move. In a horoscope, the positions of the planets are mapped against the background of the zodiac.

"Astrologers saw the constellations as forming an imaginary belt called the zodiac."

*Each group of stars in the zodiac is **represented** by a picture, shown here in the outer ring of a zodiac wheel.*

>> **represented**—Stood for or symbolized

True or false?

Astrology claims that people's personalities are influenced by the positions of the planets at the time of birth. Some people have tried to prove whether or not this is true.

One **researcher** studied groups of well-known people. In 1991, his report was published. The results led him to believe that the positions of planets at birth did affect a person's future. For example, he found that horoscopes of sports champions tended to show the planet Mars in a strong position.

A different result

In 1958, a different group of researchers began a study of 2,000 people. Most of these people were born within minutes of each other. Fifty years later, the research failed to show any similarities between these people.

Some research suggests that the position of planet Mars at birth could affect a person's success in sports.

This picture shows the great fire that destroyed a large part of London in 1666.

William Lilly

William Lilly (1602–1681) was a famous English astrologer who made many prophecies. One prophecy in particular made him very famous. In 1648, Lilly wrote that the year 1665 would be very bad for London.

In 1651, Lilly published two pictures to show what London could expect. One showed corpses wrapped in **shrouds** and men digging graves. The other showed people fighting a huge fire.

In 1665, London was hit by a terrible disease known as the plague. Thousands of people died. This was followed in 1666 by the Great Fire of London. The fire, said to have started in a bakery, quickly spread from house to house. It destroyed most of the city center.

How Strange...

Some people thought that William Lilly might have started the Great Fire of London himself to make his prediction come true.

24   >> **shroud**—A cloth or sheet used to wrap a body before burial

White House astrologer

Nancy Reagan, wife of President Ronald Reagan, took advice from San Francisco astrologer Joan Quigley. Mrs. Reagan would phone the astrologer with the President's **schedule**. She would ask which dates were safe and which were dangerous. Mrs. Reagan would try to change the plans according to what Joan Quigley said.

When news of this became public, newspapers printed headlines such as "Astrologer runs the White House." But Quigley commented, "An astrologer just picks the best time to do something that someone else has already planned to do."

"'An astrologer just picks the best time to do something...'"

Ronald Reagan was President of the United States from 1981 to 1989. His wife Nancy, pictured with him here, often asked astrologer Joan Quigley for advice.

Hand of Fate

...Some people predict the future by looking at hands.

For centuries, people have practiced **palm** reading. Palmists study the lines and shapes of hands. They believe that the hands can show a person's character and future life.

Irishman Louis Hamon was a famous palmist. He was better known as Cheiro. In 1894, he visited the United States where newspaper reporters tested him. They asked Cheiro to study some palm prints. Cheiro said the prints belonged to a man who had got money through crime. The man had used his **profession** to do this. He would be sentenced to death, yet the prints showed he would not die that way. Instead, he would live for years in jail.

The palm prints belonged to Dr. Henry Meyer. Meyer had poisoned patients for money and was later sentenced to death. But just hours before his execution, his sentence was unexpectedly changed. Meyer lived for 15 more years in jail.

This model of a hand has the main lines of the palm marked and labeled.

>> **palm**—The inner side of the hand, between the bottom of the fingers and the wrist

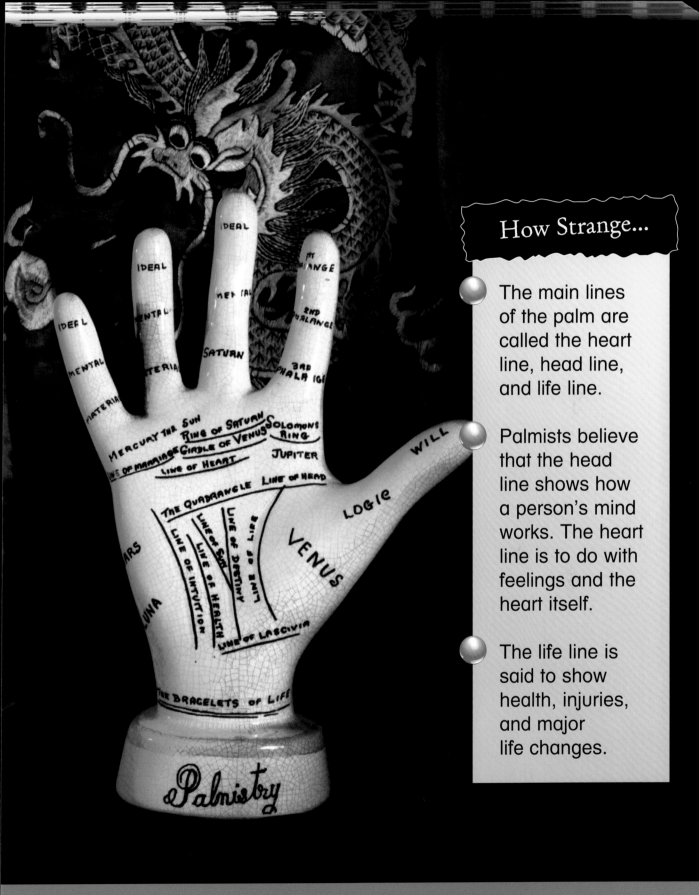

How Strange...

The main lines of the palm are called the heart line, head line, and life line.

Palmists believe that the head line shows how a person's mind works. The heart line is to do with feelings and the heart itself.

The life line is said to show health, injuries, and major life changes.

Can We See the Future?

...Maybe prophecies that come true are just good guesswork.

There are many ways in which people say they can see the future. Some read palms or use astrology. Others say they know the future through dreams, visions, or feelings.

But is it really possible to see the future? The prophecies we hear about are usually the ones that have come true. Many others do not. So could it just be a matter of chance that people sometimes get prophecies right?

It is possible to figure out some things that are likely to happen by looking at **statistics**. People who see the future say this is not how it works. But perhaps they are picking up ideas and clues without realizing. Their minds may be using this information to build a picture of future events.

How Strange...

- Jeane Dixon (see page 18) said that she sometimes used a **crystal ball** to make predictions. It helped her to concentrate on her thoughts.

- Jeane said that at other times, visions would come to her unexpectedly.

>> **statistics**—Information in the form of facts and figures

Some people say they can see visions of the future when they gaze into a crystal ball.

"The prophecies we hear about are usually the ones that have come true. Many others do not."

The idea that we may be able to see the future has troubled thinkers for centuries. If it is true, it seems that the future is fixed and we cannot change it. Or maybe, life is like a train journey. Sometimes we can see disaster ahead. Then we can decide either to stay on the train or jump off. What we do can change the rest of our lives.

Time traveling

One group of scientists believe that there may be millions of different universes. These could contain all possible pasts and futures. If this is true, some people could be able to see into the other universes at points where they connect with our own.

There is an organization in New York called the Central Premonitions **Registry**. It records and checks out predictions. The registry holds details of some very accurate predictions, often made by ordinary people. Maybe one day we will know whether predictions that come true are the result of good guesswork, chance, or something else.

> "...maybe life is like a train journey. Sometimes we can see disaster ahead."

Is the future fixed, or is life like a journey on which we can change trains?

>> **registry**—A place where information is recorded or put on a list

Glossary

anxiety Feeling uneasy or troubled

assassin Someone who carries out a murder for political reasons

bet To gamble or risk money on the result of an event or race

chart A type of map or diagram

crystal ball A glass or crystal globe that some people use to see the future

Democrat A member of the Democratic party of the United States

experience To live through or take part in something

influence The power to affect someone or something

liner A large passenger ship or aircraft

misunderstood Understood incorrectly

palm The inner side of the hand, between the bottom of the fingers and the wrist

peddler Someone who travels from house to house selling small things

prediction A warning or statement of what will happen in the future

profession A type of work that needs special training or knowledge

registry A place where information is recorded or put on a list

represented Stood for or symbolized

researcher Someone who studies a subject to find out more about it

schedule A timetable of things that need to be done

shroud A cloth or sheet used to wrap a body before burial

statistics Information in the form of facts and figures

terrorist Someone who uses violence as a political weapon

timestamped Stamped with the time and date that a letter or document is received

tragedy A shocking and very sad event

triumph Great success or victory

tyrant A cruel and unjust ruler

verse A group of lines written as poetry

waste Material that is unusable or unwanted

Index

Further Reading

• Doeden, Matt. *Nostradamus*, "Edge Books" series. Capstone Press, 2007.

• Mitton, Jacqueline. *Zodiac: Celestial Circle of the Sun*. Francis Lincoln Children's Books, 2008.

• Place, Robert M. *Astrology and Divination*, "Mysteries, Legends, and Unexplained Phenomena" series. Checkmark Books, 2008.

• Roberts, Russell. *Nostradamus*, "Biography from Ancient Civilizations" series. Mitchell Lane, 2007.

Printed in the U.S.A.